UNSUNG

MAUDLIN MONODIES

notionpress.com

UNSUNG

MAUDLIN MONODIES

JOHN
LALTLUANGLIANA

notionpress
.com

Notion Press

Old No. 38, New No. 6

McNichols Road, Chetpet

Chennai - 600 031

First Published by Notion Press 2016

ISBN 978-93-86009-44-9

Dedicated

To My Beloved Grandpa

Contents

Preface

There are some who dwell only on the present and dread the nights and the bad days. There are many who laugh at those who fall behind and get stuck on yesterday. There are some who open their eyes only to the colorful side and struggle to find joy and comfort in all that is good.

Along life's journey I learnt that both sides have to co-exist in life. It is in pain that we realize the power of healing, it is in the dark that we find comfort on a shining ray of light and it is in death that we begin our journey to eternity.

A little bit of something is what makes something else complete. Stronger is the man who walks through the fire and the storm than the one who sails on calm waters watching the bright sunny days. Badges of victories rust and die out but scars of the bravest will never fade.

The sweetest prayer comes from a broken heart than the loudest cries amidst ringing church bells. Faith in the heart of a lost traveler is stronger than the prayers chanted with ceremonial robes.

We are all a part of each other and we all a complement of each other. I have heard the whispers that were never noted, I have listened to songs that were out of tune. And it is in them that I find my strength and my lost hope.

Now it is time for me to share...

Now it is time to sing what was unsung...

Acknowledgements

A note of gratitude and thanks to my family for the support specially my siblings Henry, Rosa, Carolyn and Cindy.

Faktei, Duhsaka and Jeu Chhakchhuak for helping me proof-read my rough manuscript.

My aunt Ruth and Marina, for everything.

My friends Subi, Angha, Pubyang, Tabyo, Rehca Imchen, Angha, Bethsera Marak, Jessica Sten, Pratima, Akho, Nokchensaba, Sedevisie and all my classmates in college.

Ramenga Pachuau, Abednego Thangie and Henry for providing valuable graphic inputs.

Madam J. Longkumer, my seniors and juniors in college.

Mapuia Hmar, Annie Lego and to all who appreciated my scribblings and my small works

And to all the people I met in life who inspired me to write down these messages.

Prologue

To you who fights an endless battle
To you who is turning on a new leaf
To you who sits in silence
To you who can't let go of something
To you who holds dear to the past
To you who has a song in your heart
To you who has a story to tell
And to you, who is still on the search to find yourself...
Let this fill the missing piece,
Let this fix the broken notes
Together we will fit the missing pieces

Loneliness

Out there, stood I, in the dark
Waiting for that little spark
I closed my eyes and recalled your smile
Now I know, 'twas all a lie
I glanced up to the sky
And watched the stars pass by
I turned around
Just to count
The stars that shone in my life
Will I make it up to five?
I'll take a step but not a bet
I want to give it a try
But I just can't fly
I looked around and found
It's empty all around
The pages of my life are turning
Seconds are ticking
And I'll be here thinking
While the memories are sinking
I looked up at the grey sky once again
The stars are gone
And I'm alone

Destiny

Woke up to the sound, from somewhere near
The last few breaths of a dying soldier
Out and down in the battlefield
Left alone with his broken shield
For such was his destiny,
To die in the hands of the enemy

In the quiet corner of an empty room,
Sat an old man on a rocking chair
Gently brushing his silver hair
The face of his love has left him so
He sadly looked in the mirror once more:
And whispered, I have a hand to hold no more!"

The young boy took out his old guitar
Under the starry night, holding it tight
His only friend, besides the stars
With whom he sang the silent songs
Of broken hearts and untold feelings
Along the road of destiny, planned from above

For such is human life
Bound by choice
Yet tied to the strings of destiny
With its voice unheard
We walk unknown paths to eternity
Guided by the hands of destiny

The Lost Memory

Step out and turn around;
Take a deep breath, listen to the sound.
The cry for help, without a voice;
Feelings untold, left with no choice
Reminds me of grandma's tales,
Of trees that groan and rivers that weep
I turned my ear as the song faded
The silent chord, now strikes me deep
Felt the ground where I stood trembling
Nature now turns a toy with which we gamble
The beauty of it shrinks to just an illusion
As I stood and watched in confusion
And it is us who will pay the price
For we have rolled the dice
And played the foolish game
With nothing to bet, but shame
Tomorrow may not be mine
And how can I say 'That's fine"

This Is My Home

Sweet melody in the morning hours,
From the birds perched high on my window;
'Twas the best note to start the day with
The fragrance of the tiny flowers,
Spread vast across the bowers,
Was all it took to make my day
But now each day I awake
To the dreary silent morning
I look around and found it empty and bare
The blue sky now in shades of grey
The mystical water that once flowed
Now seems like the tears of nature
Look around and see what we have done
The place I once called heaven
Has now turned barren
Remember it's our home
We barely realize it's our own
We tend to forget that it will be gone
If we think it is for us alone

The Fall

The glory of spring and summer's noon has passed
I can feel the winter air setting in
And mother earth's call to nature
To cover her up for the coming chill
And so here they are- the fallen leaves
Covering up the ground where I stand
In hues of vibrant grey and brown

I can't seem to trace our old paths
Where we walked together in spring's full bloom
Side by side under summer's twilit dusk
Running for shelter amidst monsoon showers
And under August's mellow moon in glee
No matter where the seasons found us
My best seasons were those when you were
beside me

I can see the fallen leaves and the old barren trees
Still I can't seem to accept that you're not here
Is it already fall? 'cos I can feel autumn's breeze
I guess we have changed too, fallen somewhere
Seasons change and so do we tend to change
Along these seasons, as they come and go
Is this the pain of autumnal reminiscence?

If leaves do fall and rivers ran dry
Why do thoughts of you still linger on?
Maybe I'll wait for the next fall
To shed my thoughts of you
Or will the memories just fall back
The words we've spoken and the songs we sang?
I wish I could hold back this moment
And be with you again, this autumn

A Thousand Blooms

Have you ever heard the whispers in the wind
Of a thousand flowers being awaken by the dew
Or the ones that bend with the shadows of the setting rays?
Their songs drifting in the dull sunset tones
Dancing along with the clouds that swim the sky up high

Have you ever heard the songs from the green valleys?
Of the grasses that bend and whisper with each season
Or the songs in the woods of little things that you don't see
That's nature's sonnet in unwritten notations
And notes only the soul can hear

The Storm

I should have known that a storm was closing in
I was blinded by the sight of happy faces
And the sounds of cheerful mirth
Among them I stood in merriment
And among them I shouted in joyful noise
Little did I foresaw
That a storm was closing in

I danced to the rhythm of the gushing waves
And splashed myself in the pouring rain
I leaned forward and bended with the rushing winds
All thinking it was just a part of something great
And something to cherish and be amused with
Little did I know, that it was just the beginning
Of a storm that was closing in

Within a moment's time, I was soaked cold in the rain
And pushed to the sides by the winds
Which were no more gentle breezes
The waves have washed me now
To the shores of nothing and nowhere
And at times pull me back, to the ocean where I'm lost
Amidst the raging storm I find myself, lost

I'll drift in these troubled seas
Until the sun rises and calms the burly waters
And takes me back to the shores where I'll be safe
Or should I let myself in these waters
And let it take me away to the deep?
Where I wouldn't see or hear anymore
The raging storm that I once felt

Stars

There's a star shining bright
Sparkling in the dark horizon of the unknown
A tiny star, not many knows exist
Yet a speck of shimmer in the sky up high
Without which there'd be a space of vacant black

Dazzling below it, lays the spirit of a boy
Just one among thousands of forlorn souls
Yet one in a million you'll come across
Strong and mighty though unseen or unfelt
Here is a soul that fears no shadow

In darkest nights, stars do fade
And seem to hide in the sea of dark clouds
That hangs by and covers the sky
Yet, forever it will shine, though unseen
To guide one day, a soul that's lost

I'll be your star, shining bright
To lead the way when you're lost
To light up your spirits when the roads are gray
I'll be here forevermore
Just in case, a soul is lost

The Funeral

Tell me a story of love that was lost
Or sing to me ballads of the past
Of lovers and friends and families
That was once songs of yesterdays

I've sent you lilies for a change
They'll bloom for today and die tomorrow
They'll fade along with you the day you leave
They won't bloom forever

I'll sing you a farewell song
A funeral song to bid goodbye
Knowing I can't have your tomorrows
Why should I stay and hum a happy tune?

Memories written only to fade again
Sweet words and promises that'd only hurt again
And embraces that would only leave scars
Are these all that you've left me behind?

Laughter that would haunt me like hell
And your touch that would leave me cold
And the goodbyes that were meant for forever
Are all the memories I have of you

September

Watching the high winds pass the clouds
Up on the hill she sat, dreaming of the past
"I'd be home by September"
The words remained as clear as ever,
And the winds seemed to whisper the promises
September has already set in
And yet he wasn't back home

Summer has passed by with thoughts of him
Each day reminding her, of the promises
Like a child's undying faith and hope
She waited for the day to come
"Would you be home by winter
And tell me that September is gone?"
She whispered and nobody heard her

The sky was hazy and painted in blue
September was on the way but not him
The music of solitude filled the air
With the calm nature, humming along
She sang alone, high up on the hills,
Not really sure
If he'll be home

And then September came, in its best
"September, sweet September!"
Take me back to yesterday
And I'll wait for some more days
To watch September sky with him
But it was quiet as ever, and it was dusk
She hid her tears, under that September sky

The War Within

Greater than the wars of the world
That has been waged on the battlefields
Stronger than the fights of the bravest soldiers
And louder than the sounds of cannons
And gunshots fired a thousand times
Lies something within me
Much more than a battle

The struggle to find myself
And the battle of my emotions with my thoughts
Cuts a bruise deeper than those knives
And scars, more distinct than the soldier's pride
It's a battle that won't end
A battle of defeat each day
A battle that has no victory

Too weak to fire a shot to defend oneself
And too fragile to take one from the enemy
Such is life when it twists and turns
Faster than the way the world turns
And stronger than the forces outside
This is the battle of life
The war between me, myself and I

I broke down and wept over again
And saw the mess of the battlefield

Thinking the battle was over
Everything seemed silent and dark
But I should have known
That it was just the start
The end of the battle has just waged
Another battle

Colors of Yesterday

Under the same sky we walked
And brushed the waves of silence with our smiles
In random shades we painted our dreams;
And held on to promises whispered in unknown tones
We laughed at yesterday that was gone
And waited for the surprises of tomorrow

We built bridges of thoughts
Across oceans of life,
Not knowing what awaits on the other side
Siting by the shores and wishing
The waves would bring us back
To the sands of time

We dreamt for what was beyond
And waited for time to fly by slowly
Never wanting to let go of those moments
The magical memories captured in our minds
We counted the days and screamed out loud
For it was gone too fast

We danced with the waves and sang with the breeze
The gentle notes we learnt each day

We crossed miles and miles of hearts
And at times, sit and ponder
Over the things we did and the ones we didn't
Somewhere or the other we left a mark

The Sky and Me

He was 5, the sky was sparkling in glitters
Them spread vast in the magical night
"Twinkle Twinkle little stars"
Came the tune from the sweetest voice
Mom was beside him, the angel on earth
Singing songs that he would never forget
For the rest of his days under the sky

He was 8, the sky was blue
The wide blue canvas meant nothing
To the boy in shorts, the big dreamer
Who only thought of the big white clouds
To be the fluffy lamb from the rhymes he learnt
The rhymes that sang "Mary had a little lamb'
Whose fleece was white as snow'

He was 16, the sky was grey
It rained till dawn and on and on
The boy wondered why it rained outside
When it was raining inside of him
He had lost a part of him that night
And the sky just seemed to understand
As it sends down, showers of chilling rain

He was 22, the sky was black
He walked under the night sky
Amazed at the life he wasn't ready to face
Nothing much fascinated him anymore
Somewhere he had lost the magic
"The sky was beautiful when he was young"

On a Winter's Noon

I can see the coldness in the air
Hanging low with the fading beams
From the silent rays of the winter sun
Sending lifeless notes from the horizon
A ballad that I keep singing to myself

I'm lost in the silence of winter's noon
Faint colors and shades that seem so fragile
Spread wide in tune with the quietness
Of the lonely hearts that spells
The name of the one that winter brings forth

They sing and dance in unknown rhythm
And bring to life the pain of the past
They bring out colors and sights
That was once beautiful yesterday
But now they are just unwanted strangers

A few more hours and they'll just go down with the sun
And bring forth a dark and blinding air of nothingness
Where I see nothing, pain nor joy
But somehow my heart keeps telling me to wait
Is there something beyond these veils of uncertainties?

November Ballads

Sing to me again the songs of November
With the misty breeze like the bows of violin
And the vibrant grasses as the strings
For my mind has slipped past my soul
And missed the melody of sweet November

October came with much glee
And moments to recall and ponder
Lost was I in the old films of the season
That was played back and forth
Of the smiles and tears that autumn reminded me

November came without a warning
In silence it came and stealth
Felt its' whispers as it passed me by and left
"I'll be back someday
Look for me in the midst of the seasons"

"where was I when you came knocking?
Was I still stuck in the midst of autumn's noon?
Or dashing on to December bliss?
Wont you stay for one more time
And let me see you go?

I stretched out my arms to grab
The moments I have lost and missed
The days that were counted in silence
But December took its turn
With songs of the newborn king

Maudlin Monodies

Watching another sunset going down
with my prayers
Trying to hold back those tears I've held back
for years
Still harder it is, like the first fall...
Haunted by demons; that daylights won't chase
away
Demons from the cradle, ever alive even today
Letting go of the hurt, comes with wounding
a healed scar
Holding back the pain, kills you over and over again
Where do I keep these pains?
Where do I find solace or rest?
In the corner of my abandoned room
I found a lost doll
The one I thought could chase away my fears
She sits alone on the broken chair
Staring at one corner, calm as ever
She knows no pain, but she heals
I gave my best, I pushed myself beyond my limits
In sweat and tears, in pain
Like my mates, I grew up, securing the best
Standing on top, winning the race
Winning the fight
But you weren't there to even show a smile
I danced on my own, i rejoiced over the smallest
things

Where were you when the world saw me?
I guess you were stuck in your world, trying to find your own stage
I was invisible, I was just
Another drop in the ocean
All I ever wanted, all I ever needed,
Was for you to know,
That I was there too…
And I have been there
Praying things would change one day
Even if it takes a hundred years,
A long lost smile from the heart,
Found in the fallen rubbles,
Of the empty houses we built
Is all I ever want
I sacrificed, I bled….
Only to realise my wounds would be severed again over time
By you
The only one person I dreamt of
As the healer of my wounds and the one to hide my scars
Has now pierced it
Even scars are a dream now…
You burnt the bridges I built growing up,
Along with the little dreams I had
They'll ever remain unshared
My nights are out of stars
And my days, hidden from the sunlight
I waited for you to show me the way,

Even if you couldn't lead
But found you falling in your own pathway
Lost and confused, cursing your own
Where do you expect me to stand today?
If ever I fall again, never to rise up again
Don't come for me nor shed a tear
Cos it doesn't help to cry over a broken glass
When you saw all along that it was fragile
That first day you held it in your hands
Every day I stood there waiting in the corner
I was emptied once, drained
And maybe I'd be filled again one day I prayed
But then I grew more fragile
With the cracks growing wider every time
you came closer
Sometimes I curse the very own words I whispered;
in the dead of the night
Trying to gather faith, enough at least to believe
in myself
As I whisper Amen
Lord give me faith,
To believe in my own Amen

Platform

I'm here standing on a platform
Wishing the train I had to board never arrive
Maybe I'll spend another night waving to those on board
Until another sunrise I'll be here waiting
If ever there'll be a train,
One that would take me back to you
There's a home I prefer over the one I'm heading to
I won't mind the cold
As long as I know warmer days are waiting
Knowing you'll be there somehow
And knowing I'll be home...
Is all it takes
To keep me through the night
On this cold platform...

Purifying Flames

Upon life's hardest road I found myself
Lost in the woods, in the wild
A maze I'm stuck in,

A puzzle, without a clue.
On stranger tides I found myself drowning
Cursing the rain, every drop of it.
The waves that have sailed captains for year

Had me pulled down to the bottom
Buried in flames, burning till the last cinder.
Had me turned to ashes, down with my dreams.
The fire that burns bright for the weary traveller
Had my days turned to nights, darkest nights

I cried in doubt, sitting down beneath
Defeated by the thoughts I build upon myself
I knelt down in prayer
And that's when He spoke

In the wild, away from the things you know best
Is where you'll find me
For you have lost track of where I am
Had I sailed on without losing hope

I'd be home by the shore, waving goodbye
to the waves
"Purifying flames" He whispered to me
Burned, tested, tried and purified is gold
When it passes through the flames

Nomad

Searching for a home, a place to rest
This poor soul has wandered.
Through the desert storms and the raging winds
If only storms could break these barriers
That stands so high.
These walls stand refuge to a thousand dreams

What lies beyond these walls my soul wonders
A safe refuge or just another barrier
This life could be anything
A day older than the day lilies
Or even beyond a thousand eclipses
No one knows for sure!

Turbulent Waters

Amidst the turbulence, my soul shall stay calm
My ship might not stand the storm,
My fears might drown this sinking ship
The night is weary, but my Savior is here with me
My faith won't sink and my heart will rejoice
For He is with me amidst the turbulence
Through these troubled seas
LORD
I know You'll sail me through, safe
For once You calmed the storm
I'll sing songs of Your mercy that has sailed me this far
My heart longs for You, You're the captain of my ship
Thlipuite hau reh a
Tuifawnte thununtu nang ka nei alawm
Tiin zan mu ka chhing ang a,
Hliam zawng zawng tidam theitu,
Mittui zawng zawng hrufaitu leh

Kan lungngaihna leh tahnate
Nakina lawmnaa chantirtu tur i ni si a,
Nang lo tunge ka belh ang??

Unsung

Behind every tear lies a story,
Behind every scar, a wound once healed
Behind every victory, a battle fought
Behind every sunlight, raindrops that dried up
And behind every shower, better days
Beneath the thousand strands of silver grey hairs,
Lies wisdom through the ages
So easy it is to be lost on the surface
So hard we find, to dig deeper and search
So easy do we get stuck on what the eyes behold
Often we fail to seek with more than just the eye!
Disappointments and frustrations on the edge
The precious ones, the better ones lie hidden beneath
Away from plain sight, from the eyes
Those who dig deeper down,
miles beneath the earth to find gold and diamonds
Failed to dig deeper for what we need the most

Puzzled

Lost in the deepest embrace, a depth immeasurable at my ends
You had me captured, lurking around in circles
Wondering what comes next
With the first touch of that divine
You had me dazed in craze
Those lips that cut the deepest layer
Healed with just a single kiss
With words that wake the inner being
And words that seal the unwanted
Those meant to be forgotten

Divine Embrace

With shattered dreams I ventured into the unknown,

Clasping my tired hands, with scared knees from prayers unanswered

I waited in distress, cursing my own faith which I started to doubt

"Where's my helping hand and the promises I once believed in?'

I laughed at the souls I found singing praises; and mumbling whispers of prayers

"Foolish wishes, empty daydreams" I cried, mocking everyone that passed me by

With pride I showed my scars, and lamented over the forgotten promises.

"who do you think would hear you?"

Without a shame I trusted in my own wisdom

Not knowing it won't last

Little did I know, the day I cried and the day I burst in anger

Was a gift many others were denied of

Another day to live, be it good or bad

In the midst of deep sorrow I heard a voice

"I gave you a day, a gift not many received/

Look around and seethe flowers that blooms for a day

Many lives went by like those wild flowers that dry up

And yet you cry and complain that I wasn't looking out for you

I was there when in your joy and in your days of gloom

And you found me only in distress...

What good would it do had I made
you the happiest guy in the world...

I gave u days of weakness and flood of tears

My strength is made greatest in your weakness

A Prayer

Bound by the chains of life's uncertainties
Here I stand yet again, lamenting on what's gone
Before I say Goodbye, to all I ever had
Before I wipe away these tears,
I wanna tell you
How hard it is, to try not to love and let go
You carried me when I was like a cripple
Walked with me as I took my own pace
I walked with pride as my head stood tall
I had you beside me
And I thought I won't fall again, ever
At nights I'd lay down, counting the stars and praying
Just for you to be there, just to be there
And that's all I ever wanted
Today I won't cry like I'm the most broken,
These tears will fade, they are for a moment
I'll cherish who we have been and what we dreamt of
Along life's journey, you'll always be that special someone,
For somebody
And that's my prayer today,

For you to be the best
To be the best
For that somebody you'll meet tomorrow\

The Graveyard of Memories

There she sleeps, there she rests
Never to wake again, beneath the wild cherry blossoms
Where we once sat, under the clear August nights
I hear the promises we whispered
Blowing like a wild wind
Not knowing where to go
I wonder if you'll ever wake up just for once
And tell me of the promises we have to keep
All I ask for is a day, a moment…just for a while
To mend things right
I had words I held deep within, waiting to be spoken
Eager to be heard
As I sit here, beside you, while you sleep
Will it make sense if I whisper those words again and promise you
To keep the promises I made to you?
"I won't ever let you go" NO I won't
To some you may be gone for now
Even though you're not here now, you'll always stay
The day you slept, you were closer to me, more than ever

I had my days, waking up with thoughts of you
And my nights, in prayers
Hoping and wishing you'd be home
If only you could hear me once
And mend all the broken pieces I promised to fix
Maybe up above, someone will mend it all
I recall the nights we cried together for the things we couldn't help
Cursing life, blinded by the pain we had to overcome
We struggled, we fought and sometimes failed
But now, I see you smiling above
With hands that would never let you go
In the arms of someone
Who will love you more than any living soul ever would
BE safe
I'll be home one day too

The Lonely Pavement

Out in the cold, on a deserted pavement
I lie in wait, waiting for a shooting star
Hoping it might and fearing it won't
If I could, I would write a hundred lines,
Sing a thousand verses
But here I am, not knowing what's next.
I see souls passing by,
And no one seems to care

Watching the glitters, and the faces in glee
Like a masquerade, on a festive night
I hear the laughters, the screams, all in joy
Piled up stacks in shining wrappers
Amidst the crowd, I feel the void
Chilled by the pain of your absence
"Another year without you"

I whisper as I smile in pretense
I stare at the flames, burning away
And the faces, staring back at me
I pause and look outside the window once more, hoping
Turn my head to the door, wishing someone might turn up, knocking
I close my eyes with thoughts of you unfading

When will this nightmare end?
In a moment of silence, I blow out the candles
Close my eyes and whisper
"Happy Birthday to myself dad...
Wish you were here..."

Stand Tall

I planted a sapling, when I was young
It grew by my side, as the years passed
Under its shade, I found shelter from the storm
Beneath its canopy, I slept away the days of sun and rain
I saw the leaves when they fell,
Uncountable in numbers, like the hairs of mine that fell as I grew up
In its single solid trunk I found,
The firmest hold ever
And the strongest hug that wouldn't let go, until I did
On the harshest winter, its branches stood still
Unwritten promises that never fail
Promises of return, once spring sets in
I bid goodbye to the love I lost
Under its quiet branches I whispered them
That same old tree, where I cried over bruised knees
Only the tree kept it promises
"I'll be back in spring" I heard her whisper
I stood by it at its worst
"If at all I'll have to go first"
And my story ends before spring

I'll lie here beneath you one last time
One last time to last forever
Stand by me in my last moments
And let your blossoms fall here where I sleep
Where I'll feel safe, with no more ache

Forbidden Love

Here I am, where I'm not meant to be
A place where memories eat me away
Piles of thoughts, thoughts of you
Draining the life in me each second
This place would mean nothing
Had you not been a part of it

The songs I wrote for us remains unsung
Before I could even sing my heart out
Here goes another one, not for us, but for you
Bidding farewell to that song
And yet another farewell to who we once were
Some things are never meant to be

I lost myself creating dreams, building bridges
Bridges I thought, might lead to you
Now that it's done, I walked across it
Only to find, not a single soul on the other side
I walked back across,
Cursing the day I stopped myself
From burning down those bridges

The grasses aren't greener on the other side
Dreams and hopes proclaimed
Only to end up as childish dreams

The Captain

He has led you through the storm
Took you out from the waves
Saved you from the waves that could swallow
From the deep waters
Why do you still fear the nights?
When He who has calmed the storm
Promised to walk beside you
Through the valley of the shadow of death

Just when you thought you're walking alone
Is when he stands by your side
Watching every step you take
It is only us who fail to see
Every single step you take, He's there!

The Song

When the last friend flees and I'm robbed
Of the comfort and strength
I look to you and turn to you
When the skies turn grey
And the sun casts nothing but a shadow

When the gentle breeze gives way to the raging storm
And the ground where I stand trembles
You're my high ground where I'm safe
When words fail and the heart hurts
When everything alive turns to a void

When silence sings the victory song
You're the song in my heart
You're the melody in the glorious march
Giving one last ray of hope
To the defeated, down in the battlefields

With you, one day
I'll stand on my high ground
And the song in my heart
Will play louder
The day I triumph

Who We Are

Athletes at our desires
Handicapped to the needs of others
Blind by birth we are, to those around in need
Queens and kings of days we crown ourselves
To the needy on whose hands a few, set their eyes on

Saints and holy men we brand ourselves
To those whose sins are scarlet red,
Stained for all to see
In finest garments, gold and silver
Clinging tight to scriptures we hardly know much of
Hoping they'd clothe us, cover us
From the darkest of sins we committed

Who else but we, are the wolves in sheep's clothing?
Deaf and dumb to the soldiers of truth
Yet all ears,
To praises and false notions

Lyrical Discord

In my search for a long lost tune
Trudging along with my broken lyre
Mumbling lyrics I lost, trying to recall
On a train of discord I rode
Numbed by the unending silence
The silence that killed, the unsung melody

In my despair I searched
Stumbling along broken sheets of childhood rhymes
In the lullabies sung to an ailing child
On the farewell song for a departed soul
I found traces of the song I lost

Here I am with my broken strings
If only once, my heart would learn to sing
On dreary days and when nights are long
When the world is out of tune
And the only songs we hear are cries
Will you be my maestro?

Our songs of praises in the morn
And sweet lullabies at night
Have drowned and faded in the discord
Their melodies have morphed to random noises
What have we done, to the harmony
Of the songs in our hearts?

Troubled Seas

Dwelling on unknown waters, I strayed too long
Waving past the rescue boats like a fool
Mistaking them for empty pirate ships
Blinded by the heaps of gold, and the aroma of fine wine
Dazed I stare at the moving boats
I see them looking back, dumbfounded
A thousand hands I let go off,
A thousand boats sailed past me
I've seen ghosts and demons lurking in these waters
Here I'm sinking below, like an abandoned ship
Lured by the sea maiden's song
The song of death, the beginning of the end

'Twas yesterday I drenched myself here
Testing the depth of these unknown waters
With both crippled feet and a Confused heart
Troubled minds as my only guide
Calm and serene blue on the surface
Scarlet red deep within, is the sea I'm drowning in now
Before I sink, before another wave wash me further
I'd look for one last flag to hold on
One last boat to take me home
And when I get there, I'll be back sailing
Venturing onto unknown seas
To find and save souls that are drowning

Marionette

There she sits in the corner, in the dark
With strings attached, bind to the master's will
Her day starts and ends, when the curtains unfolds and rolls

"I'm not just a lifeless doll' she whispered
'I have danced to the tunes of the world
I jumped, I ran... I'm more than just a lifeless doll"
With the pull of a string the marionette moves
A smile forced on her face at the master's will
She smiles and frowns to the tune of the puppetmaster
"these strings that makes me move
Have strained and tied me against my will"
What was meant to ease has bound me like rusted chains"
Dragged along on the stage for all to see
Laughters and smiles I see before me
They rejoice in merriment, as I sway to the push and pull
A moment of freedom I always cherished
Once the curtains are down, and my master leaves
I sit in silence and watch the dreary day giving way to the silent night

"One day I'll break free from these strings
Be the master of my dreams
And dance to the tune of my own song

Nostalgia

Let us go back to who we once were
and dream like the child we were once
Never bothered by what awaits,
All we ever wanted, was a jar full of candies
And pockets filled with coins.

On sunny days we'd ride down the green grasses down the valleys
And our paper boats went down with our cries of joy and shouts
Down the small streams where we'd bathe in spring.
Those were the days,
When scars would heal another scar.

Take me back to that shade beneath the green grasses
Where we found comfort in nature's arms
Let the days be sunny, our playgrounds are wider
Let it shower, we'd run wild, in the pouring rain
Rain or shine, a day never went to waste

Bring me back to the innocence of my yesteryears
Dusted hands and soiled feet,
All complete with a smile that we never had to fake or force
Priceless moments, treasured dreams
Take me back, to yesterday

You Are...

You're my song in the dead of the night
When all else fail,
The melody I sing,
To help me through the empty nights
When the quietness kills, the last goodnight

When the streets are empty and none but my shadows
Walk beside me, in the quietness
You're my light, my faint ray of hope
Deep inside, a flame I hold tight
Ever burning, never fading

You're my shelter in the raging storm
That breaks my sails, that rocks my ship
My anchor on the firmest shore
The gentle waves to guide me through
You're the wind that guides my sails

On Wings

Freely I'll drift away from these pain
Up on the sky I once stared up at
Floating among the clouds,
Broken chains, broken cages
Soaring high on the wings I build for myself,
Of the feathers I grew over the years in pain

On wings I rose, wing of hope
Behind the dark clouds I see a faint ray
Reminding me of daylights
The brightest daylights after a storm
Like a thunderbird I'll rise
Beneath the storm, beneath the rain

On wings of joy I rose,
The final joy of tear, saved for the sunny day
Held back by those thousand nights of fear
Looking up at the sun I wiped my tears
Letting them go, along with my chains
Just to be another drop in the ocean

On wings of faith I glided
I may pass through another storm,
Another rain I might have to bear
Days of rain, days of sun, they'll all pass
I have my wings, never to let go
Together we will soar, up above the clouds

Old Wine

Drowning in old wine, he sings a hysterical hymn
Like a clown, dancing to a tune unfamiliar to him
He laughs at the sight of what he knows
And cries at what he fails to comprehend
Here's my world, here's my stage
Watch my story as it plays like an old film
A bottle would do to forget the bad day
Another cup of madness to end the nightmare

"There's the fool drowning in madness" they cried
Those loud whispers, the cold stares
The pain he wished he could deny
The memories he wished were erased
"Another glass, another toss, and they'll be gone"
In contentment he poured another glass
And watched the unwanted scene
Turn to a myriad of dreams only he fantasized

The likes of mannequins he saw around him
Staring with wide eyes at every move he made
Eyes locked on every move he made
Ears tuned to hear every word he mumbled
Out of curiosity, and nothing more but fun
He owned the stage, of that old deserted bar
Amidst the whispers and silent gestures
Not a soul he found, that seemed to care

The hours passed, seconds surpassed
With scenes he build with his buddy, the old wine
In the corner, a small world on his own
A forgotten mime, played over again
Displaying what was and what could have been
"I wish you knew "he whispered
And the nights drowned in the aroma
Of the old wine

Sands of Time

Standing on the shore of life's journey
I feel the waves brushing my feet
Keeping me awake, awake from my dreams
The sands of time, reminding me of castles we built
A lesson learnt, of how short our joys can last
Once the waves wash them away to nothing

Along the shores we ran chasing kites and the winds
Racing with the sailboats we built
We jumped and shouted, tears of joy streaming down
Some boats never made back home,
While some, raced as far as the eyes could see
Here I am today, sailing out on another vast ocean
Bidding goodbye to the memories I left behind at the shore

Ashes

Down from the raging fire,
Ignited from a cinder unnoticed, I burned down
With my fears glowing bright
Illuminated by the flames I set upon myself

Down to ashes I lay,
The only remnant of my troubled past
Scattered and desolated I lay
On the ground, burnt to ashes

I floated, drifted along the summer wind
Like a lone traveller, losing track
Guided by a voice within, that rings
You are dust and to dust you shall return

Yesterday I was a skyscraper, standing tall
I'd reach the stars one day
Locked away in my dreams I fell
Down to a humble heap of ash

The closest I got to the stars
Were stardusts that fell
On my cold beaten remains
Stardusts that rains on a moonlit night

To the ground under the starlit sky I rest
I'll ride the wind and float home

Or merge with these flowing streams
And be gone, to be born a new

Even stars do fall and die out
I might not shine, sparkle or glitter
Or grant your wishes like fairy dust
I'll stay here and rise again, again from the ashes

A Soldier's Prayer

To Thee I pray, my master
Before I stand on the battlefield
Before my hands are stuck to guns and cannons
Before my anger clouds my judgment
I pray to Thee,
To give me back my childhood innocence
So I'd grow tired of these guns
And for once throw them away
Like toy guns and fake bullets

To Thee I pray, the creator of life
Before my heart gets blinded by the sounds
of cannons
Before my eyes fail to see behind the red blood
stains
Before my hands move to pull these triggers again
I pray to Thee,
To take me back to my childhood days
Where I knew not who a foe was
Where I befriended all I could see
And be the best to all I met

To Thee I pray, my savior
Before I see a thousand corpses die at my hands
Before I see what you've created, being destroyed
Before I see what I'm not meant to

Take me back to my younger days
Where I knew the beauty of life
Finding joy in the tiniest creature
Finding hope in the emerging butterflies

To Thee I pray, my Lord and my God
Before I scream in the battlefield, on the high grounds
Screaming in pretense to kill the fear I have inside
Before I fire another shot, before I take a life
I couldn't create
Help me to understand the reason why I'm here
And let me win this war without guns and bullets
Help me to stand and fight the wars within us first
Those that cannons and tanks will never end
Teach us how to love, and let this madness end
With the sound of the last gunshot

The Door

I stand close to the door I once dreaded as a child
I see none but myself raising my hand to knock at it
Countless nights I've locked myself behind these walls,
Countless days I've shivered over the nights to come

Behind closed doors I've spent my years
Wasting my daylights, fighting in the dark
Scribbling broken lyrics in the shadows
Staring at the flames in a distance
Embracing the cold once more,
I mumbled words I wish I heard
I screamed in silence within,
Behind the veil of secrecy I grinned in pain
The shadows of my fears
Stand by me through the days and nights

Promise

On a long lost journey I found a lost dream
Whispering promises of yesterday in the shifting sands
I stand in awe seeing a house that stood half built
Beside it stood tall an old tree in bloom
Bearing no fruit, shedding no leaves
I saw the trunks that had made it through the storm,
The wind and the rain
I leaned closer and lay beneath its branches
And a voice whispered
"I am the promise you vowed to keep
To be back home to the one you love
To love none but her and only her
If only you knew she's waiting
Back for you, ever faithful
"I am the promise you vowed to keep
The one you whispered in your child's ear
Blowing away the candles, happy birthday
Wishing you were home, wishing you were near
Another birthday, another broken promise

I am the promise you vowed to keep
The one you whispered with a kiss
"I'll never leave you, ever"
Even the fragrance of those lips still lingers
Now they've died out, with those promises

Promises

Like a travelling gypsy I'd carry my dreams
and my promises,
Along life's uncertainties and doubts I hold fast
to them
My armour in shining shades, to help me through
the war
My faith, my ray of hope in the dark night
A thousand promises I vowed to keep
Haunting me like wild dreams, even in daylight
A word I never wanna miss, the faces I never wanna
forget
Recalling the faces I saw watching the stars
and praying
'These promises will be fulfilled one day'
Counting the stars and the days we prayed
Hoping daylights and the new dawn each day
Would come up with the fulfilment
Of the promises we made to each other
Often days would end without a sign, but
the setting sun
I could cry over the dusk crying like it's over
Or could rejoice at every dawn, waiting for the light
I'm holding on to the promise
I could believe in them or weep over it
I can only choose one, until the day we keep our
promises

Monody

A monody to my lullabies of yesterday
A farewell song, sung beneath the starlit nights
I lie awake in confusion of what was lost,
The years have blinded me,
Outnumbering my faint memories of us
I find myself whispering an old melody
Off tune and out of harmony
Another night without a song

Looking for the missing notes I drifted
Along the broken lines and the dead enchantments
In the rhymes of a child's prayer
In the noise of a crowded street
And in the dying flame and the rising waters
I find myself searching for a tune I lost
Among the fresh blooms on a sunny day
Among the fallen leaves amidst the storm
Sing to me of rainbows and fireflies
Of the shadows that fades once light sets in
Of summer and spring
Dashing through the rainy days
Awake from nightmares and demons

Sing to me a song of victory
That I may rise up and sing
The song in my heart

Raindrops

If only you'd drip and fall, like raindrops
on my hands
The likes of the ones that drain you through
Once I danced in the rain, the wild boy in shorts
Baring the cold, chasing the ripples
Little soldiers marching on through the wild
Marching to the beat of our own drummer
Singing to the music of the world we saw
We danced, we cried, we bruised, we healed
Awake at night, raindrops beating on my roof
Every drop, reminiscing the golden yesterdays
I paused and pondered, wishing I could
Go and dance in the rain once more

Epilogue

The flames will never die out
And dreams will supersede nightmares,
Scars won't last and the pages will turn
The story won't end
Here's a toss to another dawn
You and I will tell the world another story tomorrow
Another message......